Herein lies Haseena

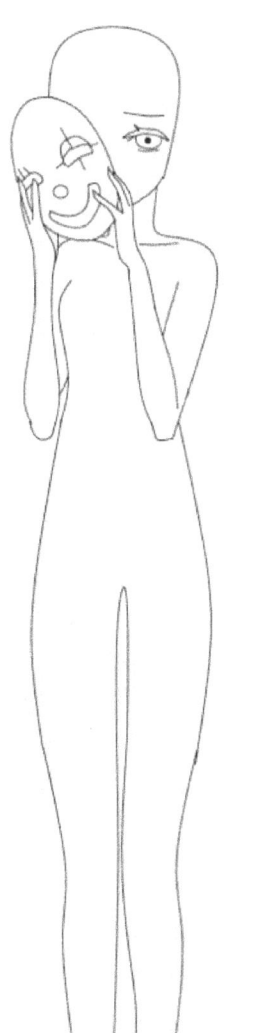

Naked and exposed...

For Andre Lefu or as I call him, 'Juju'
Who always pushed me to do this.
Rabs for being my lungs when I struggled to breathe.
Zakiya, a fallen Angel.
Rubina and Dawood, the reason I was born.
Amara, the reason I'm still alive.
My friends that always liked, read and shared
My poetry on social media.
Those guys that hurt me,
Without whom I would not have been able to
Pour out my feelings on paper.
Lastly to Conor my twin flame
For helping me to believe in love again.

Each of you, thank you

Contents

Empty pages craving for words to fill them
I stare at it until it hurts
I'm struggling to put what I feel into words
I wish I could cut my wrists
So that these words could bleed out of me
So that the pain can go away
So that everyone can know how tough it is
When you don't have a voice
Or when it refuses to come out
The life of a poet is a tough one
You're left biting your tongue
Afraid that your words might offend someone

I need to write like I need oxygen to breathe
I'm suffocating
My mind is a battlefield of thoughts fighting to come out
I'm fighting myself
Pen in hand, armed but somehow I'm still losing...

(So I will write a book where I can safely express my feelings)

"*Melancholy*"

*Forced smiles that hide a pain
residing deep inside*

I feel it in my chest and my head's a mess
Got me fighting with myself
I'm shaking
Crying
Cheeks stained
Feeling drained
I need it
I need it
They said it would be bad
These withdrawal symptoms got me going mad
I can't take it
Images of you floating around in my head
I must be hallucinating
Because I could have sworn I felt your touch
Who knew that it would hurt so much?

The sad truth is that the truth is sad

You're scared to tell people how much it hurts
So you keep it to yourself.
Choking down tears as you're forced to put on a smile
And say "no for real I'm okay", when you really aren't.
Do you know how much it hurts?
When you have to pretend to be strong
Just so that you can make it through another day.
But you don't tell anyone
Because you don't want to put your weight on their shoulders.
They say depression is real but you aren't allowed to have it.
Or you hear them say that this is
'Another attempt for affection',
Or you looking for attention
'Everyone knows that she's acting'.
So why should you say anything when they just won't get it?
They will tell you how everyone has problems
As if your problems aren't problem enough to count as problems
Because there's always someone who has it worse right?
So look on the bright side at least you're alive

But does being alive count when you're barely surviving?

It's so easy to be sad and not so easy to be happy.
I think that's why people are always on the pursuit of happiness.
But unlike happiness that you have to pursue,
Sadness just seems to find you

Visits to the hospital and it's those prescriptions again.
What can I do because they seem to ease the pain.
They say I'm losing my mind,
Well I'll tell you when I find it.
I don't even know why I'm alive, sometimes I wish I wasn't.
But there's a bigger plan and God has a purpose for each of us
But how do I believe that when my blood starts to rush.
My breathing gets heavier,
Another sleepless night, anxiety on the rise.

'Suffering from depression', they make it sound like a curse
But you know what the worst is?
Is that your life actually feels like a curse.
Can't have highs because you're always feeling low.
So you take this and that to try to numb it,
Chase the high to hide the lows,
But one day it'll change,
So I have to be optimistic.
Waiting for a day when I no longer need it
But for now let me get those prescriptions,
I really need them.

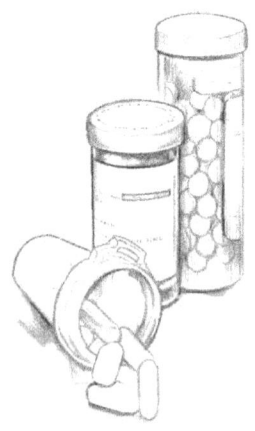

What is loneliness?

This bottomless pit of sadness
That buries away any bit of happiness
This feeling that consumes my being,
Day in and day out
I can't get out...

Even when I'm surrounded by people,
I still feel alone
I have no joy
No place to call home
Because home is where the heart is
The place where you belong

But I feel so out of place
Like a lost soul
Wandering endlessly
Begging and pleading for Death to call me
To take me home
Away from this misery

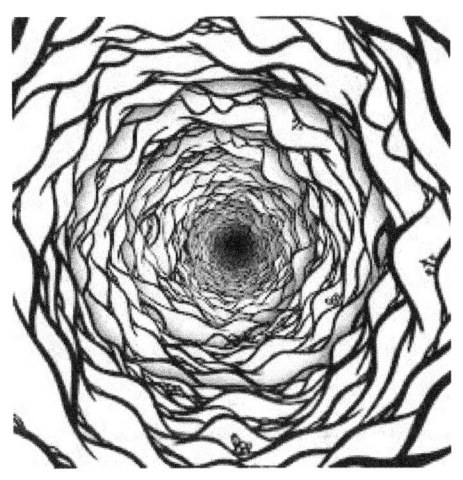

I give you the impression that I am happy
But that is just a front

Inside lies a withered soul
Inside there is no joy

I walk around laughing and joking
Whilst within I am dying and wilting

Dark days march into my life like an army
Fighting to win and take control of my happiness
Ever since it showed up, I have not been the same
My heart is constantly filled with pain
I do not want to complain
So I keep it inside and wither away
From inside, I decay

Said the blade to the wrist:
"It's been a while,
I missed you.
I miss relieving your pain
And helping you to feel better again
I've noticed that you haven't been around lately
Did you find something to replace me?

It doesn't matter, none of it does.
You're here now, that's what counts
Calm down,
Relax...
I can help you feel better.

Let me take the pain away
Like I used to.
Remember how good it felt when
I took your breath away?
I can do that for you
Relieve you from the pain once and for all
It's your call
Just take me by the hand
And let me in
I'm dying to free you."

Dealing with the pain of losing people close to me
Has made me realise that everyone I will or have ever loved
Will die and that scares me so much
That I refuse to love someone too much,
Because just as the sands run down the hour glass
When your time is up
You too will die

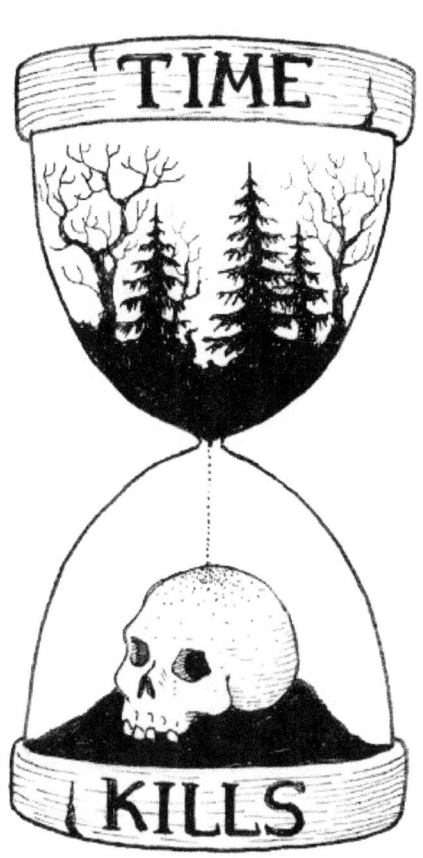

"*Anguish*"

*This hollow feeling in my heart remained long
after you went away*

Nosocomephobia

PART I

The smell of blood...
Long passages filled with suffering
Sounds of children crying in the hallway
Oxygen machines for patients struggling to breath

PART II
(Daddy)

My mind relives the day that I saw him lying there
'Both legs broken', they said
Ambulance ringing as it took us to the hospital
All alone, I sat sobbing
I took a peek in the room that he was laying in
Doctors and nurses around him
Trying to revive him

I remember the 'talk'
"I'm sorry to tell you...."
"We tried everything we could..."
And then my world turned black

PART III
(*Sister*)

When I see those machines
I am taken back to 2012
A mastectomy at age 22
I remember her smile and positive attitude
Filling that hospital room with energy that radiated

But then I remember that mask she had to wear for radiation
This was 2016
Metastasized breast cancer
Stage four
June 2017 was the day she was called back home...

PART IV
(*Mommy*)

Blood pressure dropping
She starts hallucinating
Seizures and sugar water
Back to the hospital
Diabetes is not something to play with
Drips to try to sustain her
Injections and pills
Thank God we did not lose her...

The 20th April 2016,
A day meant to be celebrated
I had just graduated,
I remember the look of pride on my mother's face
My father couldn't attend because he chose to work that day
We came back and everything was okay,
Still basking in the ambience of the day

But just as the skies turned grey,
My happiness was taken away.

In the ambulance I tried to talk to him
"Daddy, I'm here" and all I got was a nod, clearly in pain
I cried the entire way to the hospital
All alone, my sister was in a hospital too
Cancer on the brain

What do I tell my mother who already
Had so much on her plate?
We lost him at around 7 but I only saw her at 11
After spending hours filling out police reports
And answering a million questions that I had no answers to.

It was a hit and run, what more did they want?

I wanted to say sorry that I ran away
When I saw you gasping for air
Evidently taking your last breath.
And I wanted to say sorry for not telling you
What the doctors told me
Maybe if I did, you would have been better prepared.
I wanted to tell you
That I was seeing a psychologist before you died,
And how I used to cry and she told me that I was grieving you
While you were still alive.
And that ate me inside.
And I never got to tell you how hard I prayed that night,
When you couldn't sleep or breathe.
And I begged God to take me because I could feel you leaving
And all I could think about was what about your baby,
How was she going to grow up without a mother?
And what about our mother?
How could I look her in the eyes?
And tell her that the doctor told me to admit you at a hospice
But I didn't because I didn't want you to know
That you were dying.
And begged him to lie to give you false hope
Because I had hoped that it would keep you alive.
I remember thinking how were we going to survive,
You were dying
But still trying to provide for your family,
Who were doing nothing, had no source of income
And if you left what would happen to us?
And all those questions would get too much.
So I would run off looking for warmth at house number 39.
Trying to fill the void, trying to heal but I kept seeing your face
And I'd come home and stare at you,
Telling myself that I need to recall as many memories
As I could of you
Because I never wanted to forget you.
I remember my fondest memory was giving you that pedicure

And when I felt how skinny you became, my heart sunk,
And I started grieving all over again.
While still trying to remain sane and strong but I wasn't strong.
I couldn't really say anything
Because everyone would say I needed to be strong for you
And I tried
And I wished that I could have given up my life.
And I told God, I said,
'God if you need to take someone take me'
And the next morning,
He took you
And I was so defeated, felt as if my prayers were unanswered.
But still had to try to hold on
And remind myself that I knew this would happen.
But can one ever really be prepared for death?
I always said that the only certainty of life is death.
But I still felt my chest rip open and my heart breaking
Even though I knew this would happen.
Was I being silly holding onto hope?
Trying to keep my faith and praying for a miracle.
A few years later
But I still mourn you as if it just happened.
And no one knows but no one has to.
I just miss you but I'm glad to have met you.
My soldier, the embodiment of a fighter.
R.I.P you deserve peace.

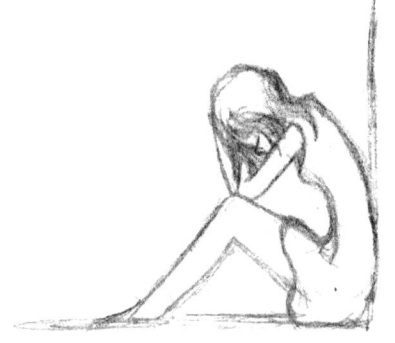

Sometimes I wish I could negotiate with death
To take me instead
To take someone who wants to die
One who has nothing to live for

I can't forget that I watched you evaporate
Into the air that winter's day when you went away.
Breath leaving your body taking my whole heart with you.

Day in and out I watched you as you were slowly fading.
Fat turning to bones, strength gradually becoming weaker.
A spirit unshaken but a body so fragile.
Eyes started sinking, heart's bleeding, hope deteriorating,
But somehow you were still smiling.

I miss you so much. I'm not the same.
I'm looking for a sister's love in friends,
I'm looking for your love in everyone I meet.
I'm trying to compensate for the pain that I feel,
Now that you're gone away.

I will never be the same,
Mourning is a part of me.
Sometimes I wish for my end
Just so that we can meet again.
I still tell you stories as if you're right beside me.
I might be losing my mind
But I feel you inside of me.
Sometimes I picture a life with you still in it.

Does the death of a loved one ever get easy?
Will I ever get over it?

A mother should not bury her children

A child should not bury her mother

A sister should not bury her siblings

A wife should not bury her husband

DEATH IS CRUEL

It takes away husbands

And breaks homes

It takes without asking

Sometimes it gives a warning

But it always leaves you empty

I'm finding it harder to ignore the fact that you're no more.
I'm finding myself reliving memories from times before.
I find myself in tears and it hurts a lot
I am a mess but I have to try my best
To be strong and hold on.
I know that you're gone home
But that doesn't make it any easier.
The pain on my chest keeps getting heavier.
I'm struggling to keep myself motivated by the fact
That you are laid to rest
That your pain and suffering has ended.
I said I love you and I meant it.
But love hurts and I can feel it.
I would have traded places with you if I could,
It would have been me not you if I could.
What I wouldn't give just for another day with you.
But I am at peace, I know that you're at ease now.
You do not have to fight anymore now.
My soldier, how brave you were.
How your smile never left your face
Not even on your deathbed.
What an amazing person you were.
I still need to get used to speaking about you in past tense,
I'm thankful to have had you as a sister and as a friend.
I will never forget you.
I can only pray to be half the woman you were
You were phenomenal.
You're where you belong now and heaven won a soldier.
Cancer didn't win, God did

Dandelions remind us that
All beautiful things come to an end
I imprinted it on my skin
So that you would only end when I do
To make you more than a memory
But forever a part of me

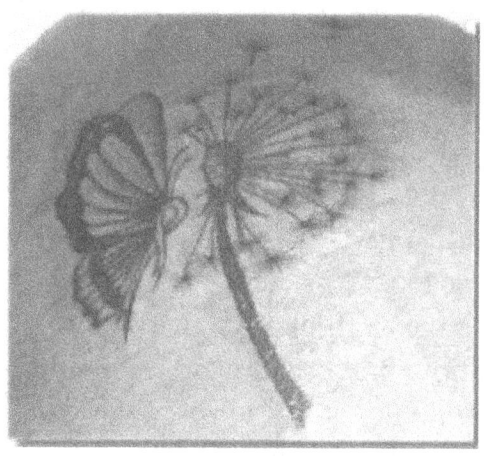

I think of you at the most random of times
Sometimes I hear something and wonder
How would you have reacted to it?
I can be in a club and the DJ puts on a new song
And I wonder if you'd dance as hard as you used to, to it
Sometimes I hear something juicy and want to tell you about it
Two of our friends are engaged now, who would have known?
Some are married now
Some divorced
There's so much that has happened since you went away
Our baby is in pre-school now
Sometimes I want to call and tell you good news
But I always pause and remind myself that,
YOU NO LONGER EXIST

But I know that you're an Angel looking down on me

In a million silent ways I mourn you.
I latch onto the feelings of memories so far gone that I fear
Will someday evaporate into the sky
And follow you to where you are.
I try to take mental pictures of things we did
When you were still here
But my emotions cloud the realities of how events unfolded.
I'm struggling to separate fact from fiction.
I guess it happens the more I realise that you are gone forever.
I'm trying to preserve you
But my memories fill me up with mourning.
Saudade grabs me whenever I see anything that reminds me of
How you used to be.
I wish you would come back to me.
I fear that one day I will forget.
I fear that we will stop saying your name.
I fear that you will be lost or altered in my brain.
I need you to stay the same and keep me from going insane.

"Heartache"

I miss the pieces of myself that I lost, given away to people who didn't deserve it

You said you'd help me work on my issues
And that you would be there for me,
On the days when my stars didn't shine as brightly as they did
When you first met me.
You said you'd love me harder on the days
When I felt like the world had let me down.
You promised to be strong for me on days when I was weak.
But you let me down.
The minute my fire died down and my leaves started falling,
You left me
Like how the winds blow down the leaves in autumn,

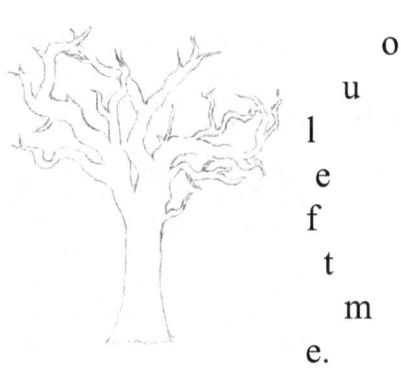

Y
o
u
l
e
f
t
m
e.

Exposed, vulnerable and alone
But I want you to know after the autumn has left
And winter has teared my last leaves down,
Spring will come and don't come back
When new leaves start growing,
And I start to blossom
Because I would have forgotten you,
As you have forgotten me.

An eye for eye will leave us both blind,
Trying to hurt you like you hurt me but what will I find?
Misery loves company so many clichés in these lines
Do to you what you did to me, but still the pain resides
It's crazy we hurt those that we love and love those that hurt us
And revenge is the dessert for the day, so it has to be cold right?
When love meets lies and tears, cheap thrills,
Lipstick stains on strangers lips to fill the void
But there's always a void.
Can't be spiteful and in love.
Can't be in love with lies,
Can't have love and no lies?
My mind's all over the place trying to make sense of all this.
Passion and pain, anger and rage,
And why am I naked on your chest again
With tears falling down?
Scared to lose you but still choosing to risk you
To test this love
Vengeance, revenge and spite, the cycle of love
"The ride of your life", that's what he said
So I gotta put my safety belt on tight
But I said that I trust you
How foolish of me for giving so much power to one person
Hoping that he'd never hurt me
But if he does, I'm covered,
Got ten fingers full of numbers that I can call
And shoulders to cry on
But why would I need to take out insurance
To replace reassurance
When he said that he'd never hurt me.
But they all do, they always do
So better to have a backup plan to fall back on
Than to be heartbroken and alone

I put you before me and made sure that you felt love.
I lifted you up even when my spirits were down.
I was down for you when no one else was around.
I kept you grounded and motivated even when I felt defeated.
And while you were floating from all the love that I gave you
You never knew that I was drowning.

You were supposed to be different because good guys usually are
They don't tell you to watch out for the good guy
The one with the pretty smile.
The one that will hurt you with a little white lie
Or a sad story or something
That will have you feeling sorry for him but he hurt you
But poets will break your heart just as bad boys will
Doctors will break your heart even if they're meant to heal
Lawyers will tell you beautiful lies that you need to hear,
Pleading his case before the jury and everyone will believe it
And turn a victim into a suspect because that's what he's good at
And writers will hurt you
And write lines telling you that he's sorry
And you will believe it because you believe in words
Until you stop
And start looking for actions
But a plumber will hurt you
By laying pipe in some other girl's house
Even a gardener will hurt you when he realises that
'The grass is greener on the other side'
So how dare you tell me that not all men are the same
When every guy I get, ends up hurting me?

Teach me to trust that there is a man out there...
Wait there are tons of men out there
But my problem is that I just don't know who to trust

The sounds of my voice got lost in the corners of the walls
And no one could hear me scream.
He choked me while staring me dead in the eyes
Telling me how he always wanted me.
I felt his strong body and his elongated manhood
Pierced a wound straight through my heart.
I always thought maybe I should give him a chance
Maybe that's why I felt like it was my fault
That we ended up on that bed in that hotel room
Even though the voices in my head
Tried to warn me not to go
But I didn't listen because
"Come on I'm single, he's nice, he's rich,
All my friends know him,
My friends know that I'm here"

And I mean when I think about it,
We shared a meal, we prayed,
We laid in bed together and made out
I allowed him to touch me
I allowed his hands to search my body
And maybe I was hurting because
I had just lost someone that I loved
Maybe I wanted to feel something
Maybe I convinced myself that it was okay
Or maybe I kept replaying the fact
That he had a gun inside the safe
Maybe I thought that it was safe or maybe I was weak
Maybe I can go through every possible "maybe" there is,
But it still won't make it right.

His sweaty body over me telling me how he likes it rough,
How he fights when he "makes love"
Ironic that he said, "make love" but it felt like war.
I felt my body pushing him out,
Trying to fight back until it just gave in
And that made him think I was okay with it
And that I wanted it.
I remember the time I moaned,
The time I tried to enjoy it
Because if I didn't, then I knew what that would make it
And I didn't want to be that girl.
But why is it that I cried so hard when I got home?
Why was it breaking my heart?
Why did I feel dirty?
Why did I feel unworthy?

*I guess my muffled screams and my cries and everything that
happened that should just remain trapped behind those four
walls*

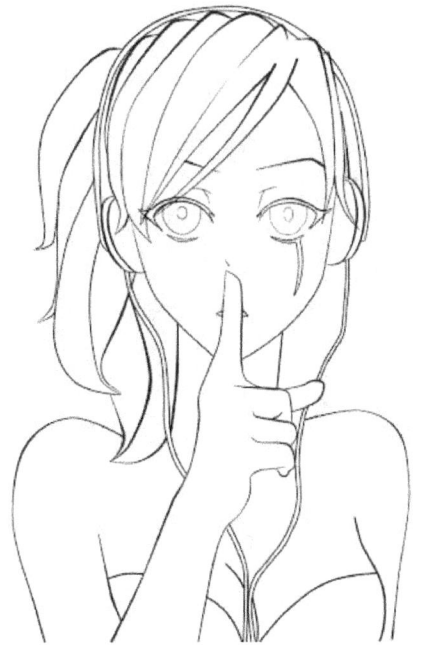

I thought I knew you,
I remember those talks late at night in between kisses and fights
When you opened up to me about what keeps you up late at night
And when you told me stories about your family and your dad
And how you loved him even when he went off his head
And when things were tough at home
And how you struggled fitting in
And how bad times were growing up
And then you gave me your diary
Almost as if you wanted me to catch a glimpse of your childhood
And see life through the eyes of a child, a teenager,
Your first crush,
When you got your heart crushed, your first love,
The years that you spent with her.
When you started coming up and how girls were after you
And you told me things about you that I thought only I knew
And I felt myself fall in love with you
Until I realised that I never really knew you...

Who knew there were two sides of you?

Enter the 'fuck boy'
The guy that does anything for his friends' approval
The guy who had to fit in
The guy with confidence unshaken,
With bad girls lining up to taste him
"Mr steal your girl"
And all the time I was living a lie.

The guy who I thought you were
Was nothing like the guy you were in front of people.
I thought I knew you, turns out I was fooled.

I fell in love with an actor.
One that knew exactly what to say
Depending on the way the story went.
No one knows the real you and
I'm starting to think, neither do you.

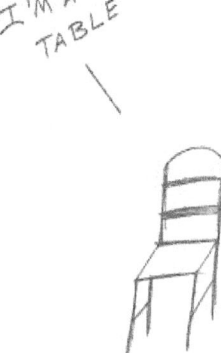

I'M A
TABLE

Identity Crisis

I tried to tell my colleague about all the times
When you were there for me and I laughed
When I realised that all the times that
I believed you were there,
I was the one that placed you there.
Everything that you were,
Was only what I had convinced myself, you were.
But it was not who you really are.

I poured all of myself into you
So forgive me if you see me looking dehydrated

Love and I aren't on speaking terms
I told it to stay away from me for a while
Because I cannot deal with another lie
But "love doesn't lie", they say
Then maybe everyone that has ever told me
That they loved me,
Weren't lying
But if they weren't lying
Why are they not here right now?

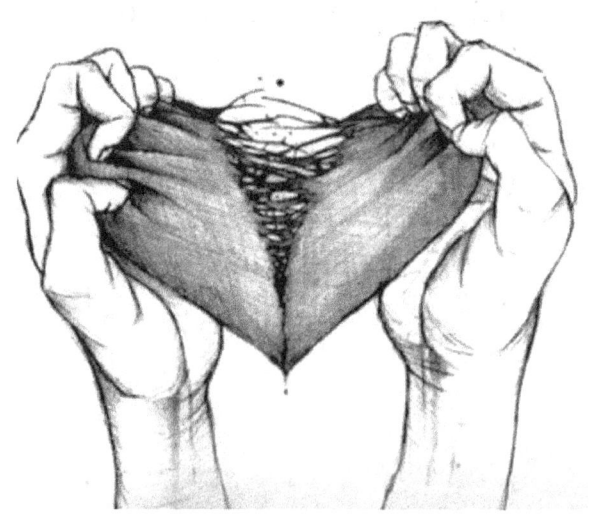

It gives me joy that my body no longer looks the same
As when you left it
And that you no longer know the person underneath it.

I painted you in bright colours
And made you appear full of life
When all that you really were
Was a faded shade of black
And tiny bits of grey

Sometimes I look for you
In the pages of your old diary
Hoping to find you
Before you got so lost
That you were no longer yourself

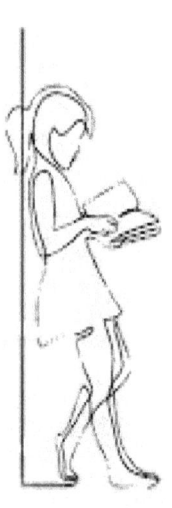

You can delete the pictures and chats
And remove me from every social media platform.
But you will never be able to erase
The way my hands felt pressed on your back,
When you were deep inside me.
You can change the sheets
But your bed will remind you of how I used to hold you
While you were asleep.
She will try to wash off traces of me
From every piece of clothing that you own,
But my scent won't fade away.
Your body will quiver when she touches you
And you realize that she doesn't stroke you the way I used to.
Tell me how can you rid yourself of me,
When my laughter still lingers in the top corners
Of your bedroom walls?

This is my apology to myself.

I'm sorry I went to that guy's house
When I felt you telling me not to go
I'm sorry for flirting with that married man
When you told me not to
I'm sorry for going back to that ex
That left me for another girl
When you told me not to
I'm sorry for sacrificing my health
For someone that was clearly making me sick
I'm sorry for forgiving him when I realised what he did.
I'm sorry for that day at that hotel room
When I let that guy violate me
Even though I told him to stop
And when he refused to,
I just told myself to be strong and let it happen
And I didn't do more than that.
I'm sorry for being weak at my own expense.
I'm sorry for putting me second
In almost every relationship that I've ever been in.
I'm sorry for not loving myself enough
To walk away from toxic situations
And I'm sorry for loving other people more than me.
I'm sorry.
But I promise to love myself first
To love myself more
To love myself hard
And not to love any other person more than I love myself.

Tonight I felt my chest tighten as I let go of the last traces
That I had left of you.
It felt as if the last of my breath
Was violently kicked out of me
And as I laid there in my own blood
Watching my life slip away from me,
I went into the light and guess what?
I saw the light.
I did not die by letting you go.
For the first time I felt alive,
Like a new-born coming into a new world
And I am okay.
These are not tears of pain but tears of joy
Because I knew that I had to let you go and that it is okay.
So goodbye, I have no more tears left to cry.
Watch as I welcome newness into my life.

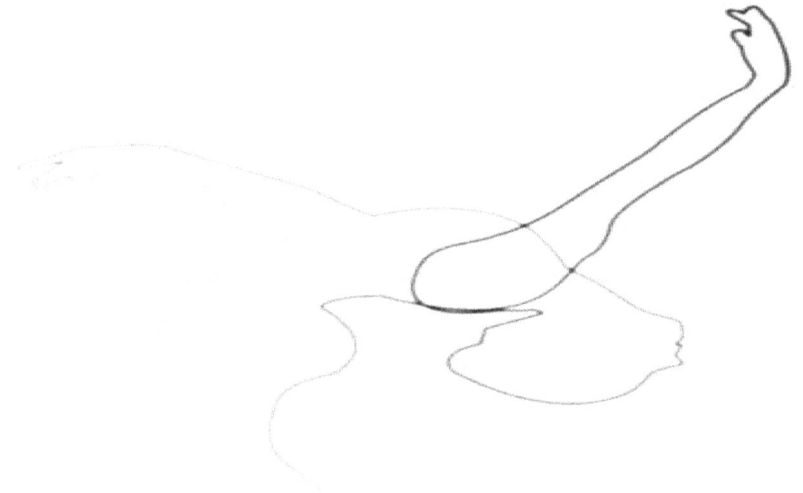

"*Contentiousness*"

Perception is bias and common sense isn't common at all

Hypocrites, that's what we are!
I always used to say that, "I'm a series of contradictions"
Make it sound smart, dress it up but deep down I'm a hypocrite.
Saying one thing but doing another
Being able to differentiate between right and wrong
But still choosing the latter.
Complaining when things go wrong but I'm the cause of it all,
For my foolish decisions.
"Wise" to some but somehow always going for the wrong one.
Preaching values but never really practicing them,
Telling people not to settle for less but then doing the same.
It's strange how I always seem to go against what I believe in.
Giving in to things that go against my beliefs
And then trying to justify it in my head
Because I'm only human
Because "YOLO"
Because this and that
And it's making me mad
And the worst part is that I know better
But I still fall for the same traps that I set for myself
It's a joke really when I think about it
Although there's nothing funny about it.
See hypocrisy
Irony
And me?
Still a series of controversy or wait,
Wasn't it contradictions?

Many times we expect people to think the way that we do
We're under the impression
That because we view things a certain way
That everyone does or should too
This is wrong of us
Because everyone has their own way of viewing things
Then we get upset because we assume that our way of thinking
Is the universal way
But in actuality, it's not
We are all different and sometimes we were raised differently
So that also influences how we see or do things
I've learned to try to understand why people do what they do
Instead of saying what they're doing is wrong
Because sometimes they might not think of it as wrong

They want to open you up like the pages of a book
But some of them cannot read
And the rest do not like the content

Does love have a button that you can switch on or off
Depending on the situation?
Like when she switches it off and puts on her heels,
Dressed to kill,
Wearing clothes that he barely sees her in,
Smelling so fresh and so clean
On her way out to sin.
Comes back smelling like gin.
Its 3am he's fast asleep,
She switches on the love,
Opens up the cheats and climbs in besides him.

Love can be turned off,
Like when he turns you off
By the way he always lays on the couch,
Hand on his crotch,
Not lifting a finger to help in the house
And bills pile up and they cut the power out
And you just hate how he doesn't give a fuck.
But you stay around
Because when you turn the love back on,
You remember that he was the one,
So you switch it on and forget the flaws
Look past the imperfections
Because love was never meant to be perfect.

Part I

As I walk down that hallway making my way to the room,
I swear I could hear and feel both our heartbeats.
I closed my ears to block out the sound of you
Crying from within me.
You probably hate me, I cannot blame you.
But I am saving you, saving you from me,
From cruelty, from the pains of this world.
Can't you feel from within me, the love that I have for you?
But you were made by two so where is the other?
Well he was not ready to be a father and I know that I'm no better
But I would rather let you go and be with an eternal Father
That will love you.
I know that I will be judged, called a "murderer" perhaps
But I'm saving you
Saving what's left
So that you don't have to grow up in a home
Where your parent is unknown
Where there is struggle and pain
I would rather die than let you go through life roughly.
It's never been easy
Please baby don't cry,
I can't take the sounds of your unborn cries.
They will judge me but they have no idea
How hard this decision was.
I see the room, I see the bed,
Soon my baby this will come to an end
And I can only hope you forgive me.
Maybe someday I will forgive myself!

Part II

As I hide away in my room I can hear them,
There they go fighting again.
In my 13 years of being here
I've heard more "I hate you's" to last a lifetime
I don't mind, I guess I'm just too tired to try to understand
Why or how could two people that once loved each other,
Not be able to stand each other
I see the pictures on the wall but pictures lie
Maybe they never loved each other
Or maybe I'm the reason why.
Could it be that after me, they realized it wasn't meant to be?
That maybe I am the cause of their pain, their anger, their fury
I hear them speaking about divorce,
I guess it could have been worse?
But what's worse than a divorce?
Am I selfish for wanting them to try and make it work?
So that I can have a happy family?
But they are not happy and I hate it.
I guess I'm going to be another statistic
Another child whose parents did not make it.
So unfair because all I wanted was to feel care and love
But this fighting is too much.
I know I'm the reason and that hurts a lot.
I wish I were never born.

Part III

As I sit down with the needle in my hand,
A million images play around in my head.
I cannot sit down, I think I should stand
You see these pills got me on an edge and
I keep seeing these damn images in my head
And I need this, I need to "fix" this.
This fix will fix this.
I don't expect you to understand,
I'm just a "junkie", a "druggie",
But you don't know how hard this is for me.
You think it's easy, stealing from people that love me,
Hurting the people that care about me.
Do you think I enjoy seeing the disappointment on their faces?
When I come back from rehab,
Only to relapse and I'm back at it again.
But it owns me, I no longer control me,
It has a hold on me, it does!
I know it's easy for you to say "that's enough, stop it now",
But I do not know how to
So I remain misunderstood

Part IV

I look down at my slit wrists
And as the blood rushed out,
I could feel it
No pain, just a flow of emotions.
See no one knows that I fantasize about suicide
And how it would be, if there was no me.
No one would blame me,
Or hurt me or try to change me
Or mould me into what they want me to be.
I would be free, and this fantasy drives me,
It's the fuel that keeps my engine going.
Fuels and engines
Mmm isn't that a way to end this all,
Poisonous fumes?
Maybe a rope would do.
Tie it around my neck and just step back
And fall into infinity.
I wonder if they would miss me.
Take some responsibility,
You did this, not me.
All I wanted was for you to love me,
Wait, I think I just cut myself too deep
But I didn't even feel it.
Who knew dying would be so pain free.

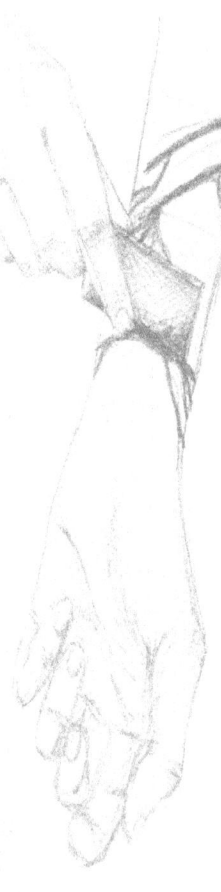

Part V

As I lay here next to her all I can feel is love
How can they say that this love is lust?
Being a girl that's in love with a girl
That means the world to me, happens to be a sin.
A sin that cost me my family, they cannot accept me.
They said that I made God angry
Yet He created me in His image
Am I being disrespectful for saying I see Him in me and in her?
Why would He allow that?
Why would He place these feelings inside my soul?
And create someone that makes me feel whole
But then have people tell me that she's not made for me.
Yet there is someone for everyone
But it just so happens that it changes for lesbians
Maybe I should rephrase that "*there is a man for every woman*",
But who said that?
How is it okay for you to judge me by my "sins?"
As though you are without one.
So murder is fine, even raping an innocent child
But two people being happy and in love
'Oh my! That's the greatest sin of all'.
For too long I hid away in that closet
But I've outgrown it
And I'm starting to stick out so I won't hide anymore
It's a pity that I have to justify who I love, defend my choices
But I'll do it because she is worth it.

Part VI

As my lifeless half developed body is laid to rest
I wish people could understand that moms know best.
She knew that my life would be a misery
She knew that this was meant to be.

As I went up to heaven I cried, I didn't want to die.
But I couldn't be the reason
Why my mother had to cry herself to sleep every night
Because she feared for her life
And people telling her to do what's "right".
I understand God had a better plan.
He knew that she wouldn't be able to take of me,
You see little bodies need a lot of things
And she wouldn't be able to provide for me.

Mommy I'm not angry I heard how he treated you
Made you feel like you had trapped him into making me
And I wouldn't let you keep me if he hated you because of me.
Mommy I forgive you, I just wish you knew that I do.

We men think that it's okay to treat our women poorly
We men forget that it was in the bodies of these
Women that we were moulded
Kept protected, nurtured and alive

We men think that it is okay for us to hurt our women
For us to call authority over them
For us to take their voices away
Silence them
Force them to be quiet about the things that
We men put them through
We men forget that it was women that gave us our voices

We men rip from them the very homes that kept us safe
We men think that it's okay to treat women like they're
nothing
Because we're men and we can get away with anything

WOMEN RISE UP TO THESE MEN
Don't allow them to silence you
To make you a mute
Another statistic

"Confusion"

My body and my mind
are at war with each other

You, Wrong
You sneak into my life
Like a thief in the night
Robbing me of my light
Bringing your darkness
Exposing my weakness
Feeding on my loneliness
Filling me up with false happiness

You, Wrong
You show up in my life
Draped in jewels and pearls
Fully knowing that I will
Be dazzled by your beauty
And foolishly
Give you all of me

You, Wrong
You appear in my life
Changing my perception
Bringing feelings of sensation
Persuading me to change direction

Oh Wrong
If only you knew
I have to resist you because
I can see right through you
You're no good

Will I ever be ready to commit myself completely?
Scared that these issues go so deep
That I will never really open up.
Afraid to receive love, say I don't believe in love,
Loathe it
Hate it
But even hate stems from love
And it all goes back to the reason why we are alive.
Made to love, created for love
But what happens if you don't believe it?
Like an atheist that doesn't believe in God
I fail to see love as this beautiful thing that gives us hope,
Or a reason for breathing.
To me it's just a hoax,
An abstract concept created by men
To cure a loneliness that they created.
They'll call this blasphemy but I don't mind it.
Love is an illusion

Wanted to write a poem about love
But then I realised that I don't understand it

You put your mouth over my funnel
And start to drink from me
As if you had been in the desert for too long
You drink and drink
Your thirst is insatiable
You drink from me as if to fill yourself up
I never knew you were this empty
That you come to me looking for a way to be whole again
My body is your salvation
But it's a pity that you couldn't save me

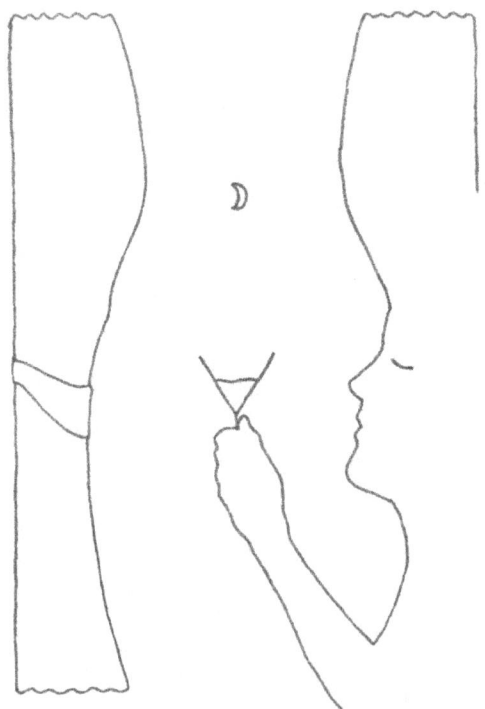

Love came to visit me today dressed for the occasion.
He took me out where we dined
And I whined and complained about everything that I hated.
He tried to wrap his arms around but it was rejected
Because I lack trust
And I hate the way that Love makes me feel.
So weak, so needy,
And I remember the days when I loved Love
But now I barely like him.
Love and I have a love-hate relationship
Okay maybe I don't hate him
But I can't stand the way he looks at me
I know that this disappoints him because he hardly gets rejected.
He always gets his way, that's what's expected.
He tells me his over rehearsed lines that I know are lies
And he tells me his goals, his dreams
And it's meant to warm my soul
But this ice box that replaces my heart
Needs more than warm words
Or talks under blankets or bonding.
I know I said I'd give Love another try but I lied.
I'm not ready to lose myself for Love
I'm not ready to give him that power
But somehow he doesn't give up
He has faith that he is enough
Unfortunately Love is never enough

Proverbs

1. Love is a choice

2. Respect is deeper than love

3. Love is tolerance

4. Unrequited love is love wasted

5. Love and Logic are like oil and water
   They don't go well together

6. We want to be loved according to our terms
   By people who don't bother to read the terms and conditions

There's no such thing as an unconditional love
It's always 'I love you BUT'.
And if they don't tell you the 'but',
Then someone else is hearing it

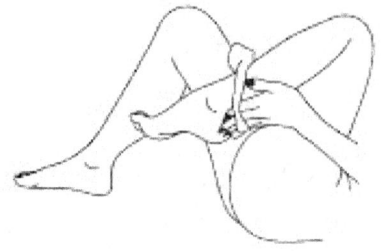

We do not love each other
So tell me how did I end up on your bed?
Using my vagina to think and not my head
See I'm so scared of opening up
That I'd rather give up my body
Instead of my heart

Sex is easy, love is hard

3am and I'm knocking on your front door
Everyone has an addiction, something to ease the pain
It's funny that mine happens to be your body
I don't love you
I just love the way you make me forget

Been blunting a lot lately,
Drinking a lot lately,
Talking to way too many boys lately
Searching for a feeling
For meaning in places that offer temporary thrills
Getting high to hide the lows
Going out partying every other night
Scared to be alone
Hiding away from thoughts
Ducking memories
Trying to conceal any feeling of what used to be
Trying to forget the who, when, what, why
And how did it get to this point?
Nobody ever seems to know
But somehow everyone has a story

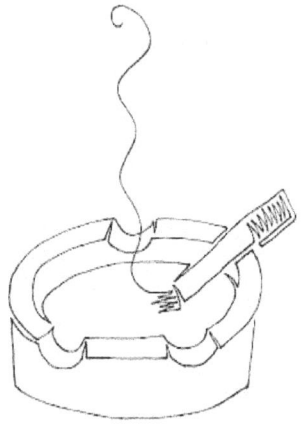

They love your hair
Your African body
Your big butt
That's why they think
That they can love you
As if your body makes you,
YOU

We're just two lost souls

Looking for somewhere to call home

So we rest our heads on different beds

Longing for belonging

But we were never meant to be

"Cravings"

Give me something to cure this hunger

Two hungry souls

Laying entwined in unison

Embracing in intimacy

The bond of hearts

Bound in oneness

The power of two

As One

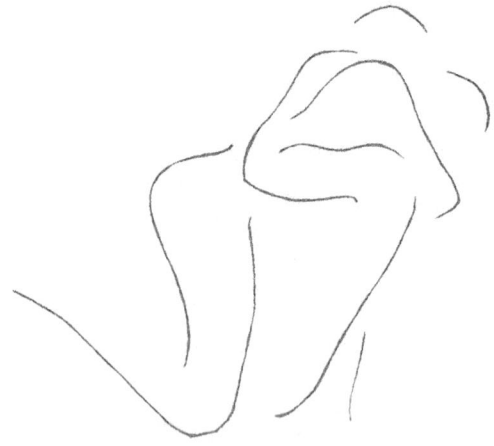

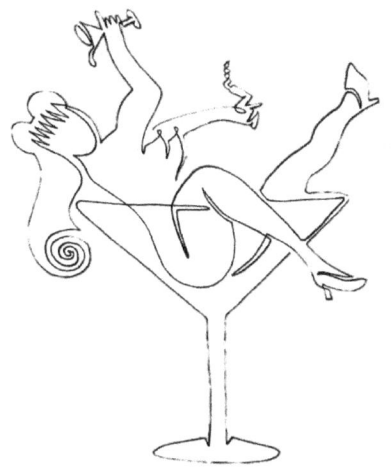

Woke up this morning to flashbacks of last night
Sweaty palms pressed against backs and breasts,
Fingers tangled in messy hair
Warm breath caressing ear lobes,
Ash and bottle caps, bottles and cigarettes
c l o t h e s s c a t t e r e d o n t h e f l o o r.
Laughter and tickles that turned to eyes
Staring deep into each other…

You move to the sounds of drum beats
I move to the sounds of an acoustic guitar
Our rhythms meant to be one
But our bodies move in separate flows

My energy is slow, low, sensual, and passionate
But you, you're rushing, racing
And I cannot keep up

You need to relax
I assure you, I'm not going anywhere
Take your time...

I struggle to understand your rush
Your furious thrusts
STOP!
This is enough

Our bodies are meant to be creating harmonies, melodies
Not some 'battle of the bands'
Intertwined,
Let our rhythms be as one

Calm down
Let my movements, move you
See,
No rush

Allow your body to move to my beat
My flow
And you will feel us cum together
Like a well put song
With no words
Just mmmms and yeahs

Softly, a cool breeze passes through the small space
Between your face and mine
Suddenly, it feels as though there is a pause in time
Slowly, I feel you come closer and closer
I feel my heart start pounding,
Heavier,
Faster...
My eyes shut tightly
I feel you put your arms around me
Immediately, I realise that I'm right where I should be
Gently, I feel your lips suppressing mine
So tender
So kind
Oh what a feeling I never knew
Felt magical but yet so true

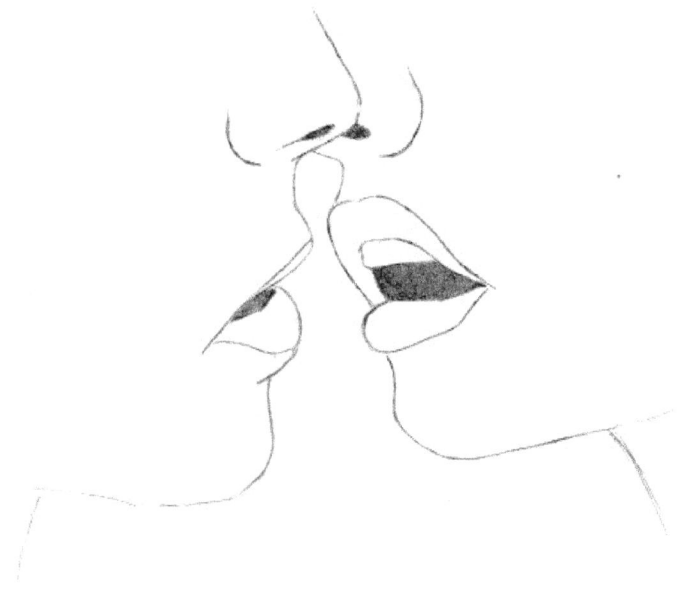

It's more than sex with you
Our bodies tell each other stories
As if they had been away for too long
They speak in a language only known to them
They speak in touch, movements and moans
How is it that when we're bound together
It feels as if we're filling each other up?
Like pieces of a puzzle
You fit perfectly inside me

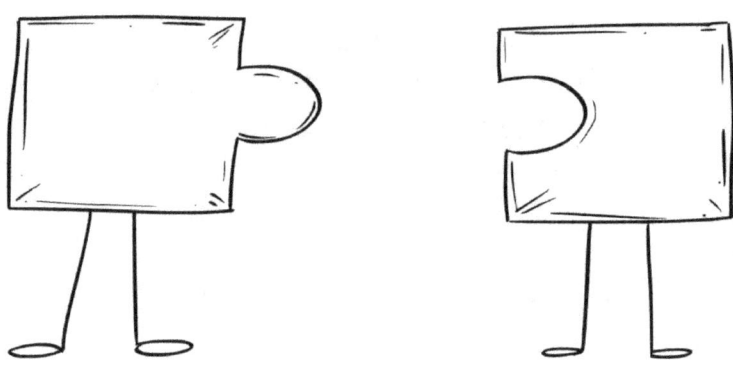

I feel you journey down my body
Dropping kisses all over, as if my legs would get jealous
If you didn't kiss them too

You own me
You own this body

The way it listens to you
Doing exactly what you want it to

It's raining indoors
You manage to turn storms between my thighs

You licked your fingers and then began paging
Through each section of my body

Undressing me slowly,
I see you searching for the real me
Underneath these clothes
Taking off each layer, cautiously,
Kissing me softly on the places that I said he hurt me
You trying to heal me,
To make whole what was taken away from me
How do I tell you that I need more
Than your hands on me to complete me?
How do I tell you that sex won't heal me?
It broke me
It takes more than thrusts for me to trust
It's not your fault that sometimes my eyes fill with tears
When you're on top of me
I just can't seem to forget his face

I might be your first option
Or your last resort
But I am not the only one you turn to
When you need someone
I line up with the others
And hope that you choose me
And you know what?
Sometimes you do

I'm mistaking lust for love again.
Another love story that started on a bed.
My heart so far guarded that the only time it feels
Is when there's something inside me.
I'm confusing pillow talk for opening up,
And opening up for being naked.
And peace is found in bedsheets.
And stress is relieved in orgasms.
And I know that it's not love but it makes my face light up,
I'm glowing again.
The depression is going away again.
Sex seems to be the cure again.
So how can I not mistake it for love when it fills me up
And makes me feel like I have something to look forward to?
I'm escaping to that place again,
I'm scared because it always ends up the same,
Sex is not love,
Love is not lust,
But when you don't know what love is
It becomes easy to confuse it.
Soft kisses planted on my back while I sleep,
Hands holding me while I sleep,
Morning kisses,
It's all the things I miss so how can I not confuse it?
I know better, I've been here before
But there's something about lust that makes it feel like love.

Lust disguised itself as love so it's hard to tell them apart

"Hesitancy"

Broken hearts are filled with doubt
afraid to get hurt again

There is so much that I would like to say to you,
So much that I wish you knew
But every time I speak to you,
I choke
These words fall out of my mouth like an actress reading a script
I convince you what I say is true
Like when you ask "How are you" and I say "I'm okay"
But if only you knew what I truly feel
Then you would know that it's real
But I hide it,
Disguise it,
Keep it hidden so far inside in hope that you may never find it
Because I fear you
I fear what you would do if you knew
I fear me
See there's a difference between dreams and reality
And in my heart I created an image of what could be
But that was easy
Actually I have no idea nor certainty that you are what I need
That scares me
How do I open up to you and let you know what I feel
When I don't even know what the deal is?
I feel for you that much is true
But you do not show me if you're feeling it too
So I can't risk it
I keep my feelings sheltered and act as if it does not matter,
I guess it's better this way
Yes I long for a day when I can tell you what I'm feeling
But until then I will keep to acting,
Pretending that you mean nothing
When in reality you mean everything

The sad thing is that I have never ever had a love relationship
I was always the lover, the one trying to please,
Take care of and support the other
I think that is why I am hesitant when it comes to love
Because I keep giving to those that only receive
But that don't reciprocate
So excuse me if I don't know what being in love feels like
I never had the pleasure of knowing how to be loved

Funny how many forever's we go through, looking for the 'one'
So hopeful that this one will be that forever that actually lasts
And then the next one
And the next one
And it's like each one takes something,
When they end up not being the one
And when you finally find the one
You not even the same optimistic person,
You were in the first place
You're more careful with your heart,
Taking more time to open up
And then there's insecurities, trust issues and weird shit
And you still end up not being the one for your one
And then end up having to go through that same cycle
Of finding the one...
It's a tedious process until you actually find that one forever
That becomes your forever... Forever!

I like how we never give up though.

Dear Crush, I hope that you read books,
And I hope that you question life.
I hope that you understand that people are different
And that you shouldn't force people to change.
I hope that you get that life can be really shitty at times
And that most times all we really need is
Someone that understands.

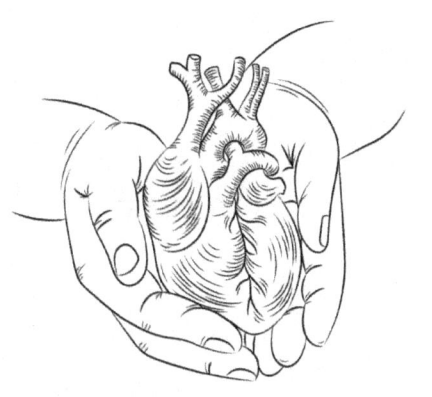

Teach me to love without fear,
Without hesitations
Without previous convictions
And tall walls guarding hearts
And all those thoughts and
insecurities.
Let me love like a child
Who has never felt pain before.
Teach me how to love
Earnestly,
Sincerely,
Easily,
Why does it have to be
complicated?
It's always 50 shades of black
Because nothing is ever clear
Nothing makes sense
But love isn't supposed to make sense
It's meant to be felt?
I want to love without boundaries,
Genuinely, like how a child loves so sweetly
Without grudges and doubt.
What is love with doubt?
Help me,
I want to love someone with all of me
Not leaving any room for disappointment,
Waiting for them to fail me.
Teach me to love without questioning intentions
And wondering if it's all a lie

No I'm not finding myself waking up on different beds,
In an attempt to forget or heal.
Looking for shoulders to cry on.
I'm not getting under someone
To get over someone else.
I'm not going to go around selling dreams
Because mine were stolen from me.
I'm not going to talk to a bunch of people,
Trying to forget that one person.
This time I'm going to take time.
I will not look for comfort in bed sheets,
Or quickies in alleys to numb the pain.
This time I'm crying about it
Instead of suppressing it.
I'm dealing with it (alone)
So that I don't lead these people on.
I'm working on me, finding healing from within.
Rebounds are fun to take the mind off things
But the heart needs to feel in order to heal
And I owe myself that.
So no more sneaking off to meet so and so
And saying half I love you's so I can be happy and forget.
This time I'm taking some much needed 'me' time
Not to be lonely, just to be alone and to grow.

There's something about something new
That makes you glow differently.
When there's a positive change in your life
Be it a new healthy relationship or new job
Or that answer to a prayer
That had you crying from within your soul
That makes you smile differently,
That makes you view life differently.
So many times we're caught up in all the bad things in our lives
That we fail to take time to realize the good things.
But a new thing is different, it comes when you least expect it
And it's a gateway for positive feelings,
It is that bounce in your step.
It is that letting go of a bad lover and getting a new haircut
It's going out and living.
It's finding your smile.
It's finding you.
It's doing you and it's beautiful.
It's a perfect feeling.
And it's a feeling that we should cherish
Before we fall back into our old ways of not counting our blessings
Or forgetting who we are and what we deserve.

No insecurities, I will not be entertaining you.
Doubt and trust issues the door is closed, please go away.
I no longer need you sitting on my shoulder
Telling me that I'm not worth it
Or that he's creeping or that he's doing anything.
I didn't ask you to keep guard for me.
I'm letting my guard down because I cannot love someone
But doubt them
Or fear them or be worried about every move they're making.
He makes me feel guarded and safe
So no I won't be entertaining my lack of faith today.
Let me have this and enjoy it my way

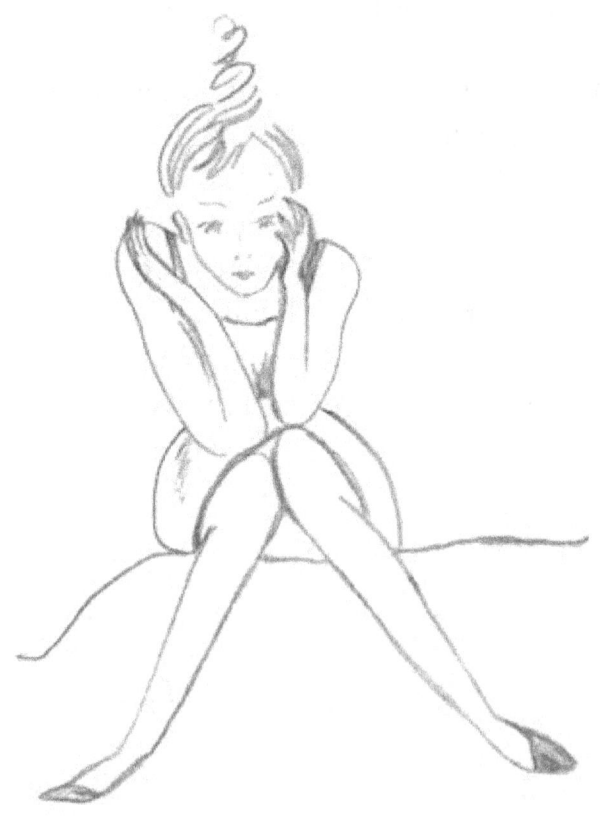

"Companionship"

Sometimes in the midst of a storm someone comes and offers you an umbrella

One day I will write a poem about a new love,
About someone who makes my face light up like a Christmas tree
Just by talking about him.
The tone of his voice will be like a Melody I had longed to hear
But got lost in the wind
Lost with lovers posing as him
And when I hear it my heart will instantly recognize it
It will complete my song that I for so long was singing off key
It will be him and I and I will have no more reasons to cry,
No more hate poetry to write about how I don't believe in love
Because then I won't just believe in love but I'll be living in love.
The embodiment of what my definition of love used to be
Before it got swept under the carpet
Or put away in boxes and stored in an attic that has no staircase
And it will make my heart race
And maybe I won't feel butterflies
But maybe, just maybe I will feel safe, content and secure
And when he holds me in his arms
I will realised that this is the one,
The one who prayed so hard for me
The reason that God could not allow me to last
With anyone before him
Because He was waiting for the right time
To introduce my 'one' to me.
Maybe when I see him my heart will know
Or maybe it will take a few bad dates, some dinner, some chats
Or maybe it will be when his hand touches mine
And it sends shivers down my spine
And I realise that chemistry is that spark you feel
When you finally meet the one.
Or when you can't put the pen down
Because you want everyone to know that
You finally got it right this time

My love is not manifested in those three words
That so carelessly runs out of mouths
And falls on ears hungry to hear it
My love shows more than it tells
My love knows that although there is power in words,
Words without action mean nothing

I will show you that I love you
Before I tell you that I do
But when I finally say it
It will be like a cherry on top of the cake

I kept staring at a blank page
Hoping that my feelings would guide me,
See I have never written about love before
Not sure if I have ever been in love before
But there's something different about you
About the way you make me feel secure
And I'm left thinking maybe that's what love is,
SECURITY
See I've had tall walls and guard rails
All around my heart
But somehow you managed to climb up
And get around it
Now there's a room that you reside in
And I don't even mind it.
You put the spring back in my step,
I wake up feeling relaxed.
Gone are those days of anxiety
Because somehow
You know how to keep me calm
And when I feel down
I know that you will be around
And I don't doubt it.
Love teaches me
How to tear the walls down,
How to open up, how to receive love.
Many times I felt that all I did
Was give love
But never really got it back
With you it's different, you reciprocate it
You never make me feel like I'm wasting it
By loving you.
I know that our love is new but somehow
I feel like I had always known it was you.

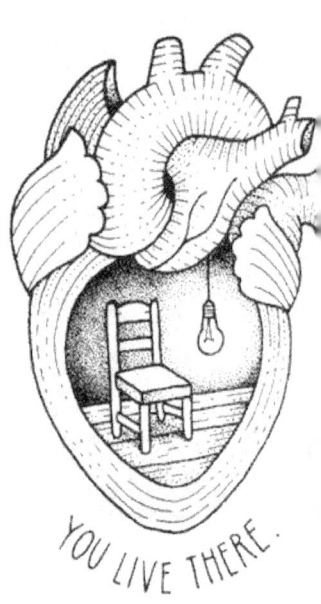

YOU LIVE THERE.

As my fragile heart cries
Choose me

As you tremble in fear
Hold me

As my insecurities rise
Help me

As my trust fades away
Find me

As your faith withers
Believe me

As my heart heals
Heal me

As you begin to find yourself
Guide me

As I become hopeful
Inspire me

As you learn to love yourself
Teach me

As we become one
Join me

As we unite
Love me

As we love
Trust me

Redefining my understanding of love.
I said love and not attachment.

I remember watching a video and the lady said,
"Attachment says I love you and therefore
I want you to make me happy
Whereas love says I love you so I want you to be happy
And if it includes me then great, if it doesn't, that's okay".
She said that love is an open palm
That allows the person to be free and be themselves,
It is not a tightly clenched fist.

Our problem is we try too hard to hold onto the ones we love
Because we're so fearful that at any time they will leave us
But we do not realise that the more tightly we hold onto them,
The less we're allowing them room to breathe.
No one wants to be in a relationship that suffocates them.

Love is not being scared to lose someone,
Love is loving someone as best as you can
And allowing them to love you back.
If they leave that is okay
At least you had given it your best and allowed them to be free.

Love treats me like I matter
He takes me out on dates unlike those before him
That only knew how to keep me trapped between bed sheets
And closed doors
He shows me off to the world
He thinks I'm beautiful
Not only externally but internally
He tells me that he has never met someone like me
To him, I'm his greatest victory
He is proud of me
As if he finally found a diamond after picking up stones

He doesn't know that he is more precious to me than gold.

Unmasking a person that wears a lot of masks,
Because they're so afraid to be vulnerable, is a difficult task.
But you peel through each layer with caution
And even though some parts make you uncomfortable,
You keep on removing them until the end.
You're patient, you don't rush trying to expose me.
But take your time discovering each side of me.

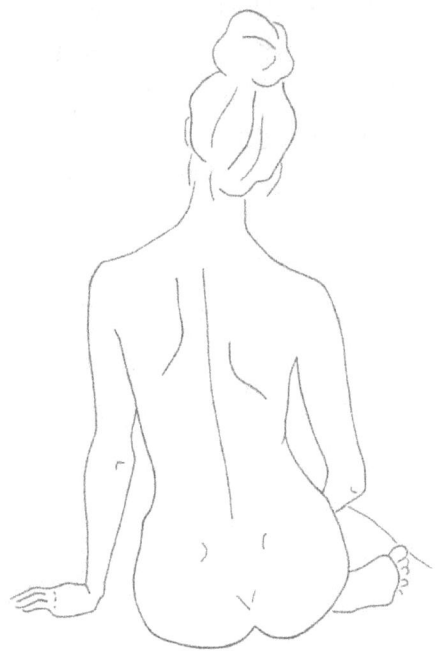

*How can I not love you, when you saw me in my nakedness
And yet still chose to love me?*

Tell me how you do it

How do you look at me with eyes
That sees deeper than my exterior?
You look at me and you see the little girl I used to be,
The young lady I was and the lady I became.
You see through my hard shell and façade

Tell me how you do it

How do you understand my language of love so immaculately
As if you studied to perfect it?
You know how to speak to me without saying anything at all
You understand me, not the pretend me but the real me

How do you do it?

I think our living room best describes our relationship.
When we stayed in two different houses,
Each of us had our own stuff.
Each object that filled our living rooms were personal items
I think of them as what made us individuals.
When we moved in together, we put his sofa next to my sofa.
His bookshelf has my TV on top of it,
My sofa has his cushions and his sofa has mine.
The bookshelf has a blend of his books and mine.
His sofa is green and mine is black but it fits so perfectly together.
The shapes are different but they both offer us comfort.
So I think in the end a relationship is,
Two people with their own "furniture"
Coming together to create a home.
I'm thankful for the home I found in you.

Thank you
Thank you for loving me when I was not that easy to love
For not giving up when I was pessimistic about love
Thank you for holding my hand
And showing me that love isn't something to be afraid of
For making me believe in love
For not making me doubt it
Or waking up in the middle of the night
To an empty side of the bed because you decided to stray
Thank you for staying
For showing me how real love is supposed to feel

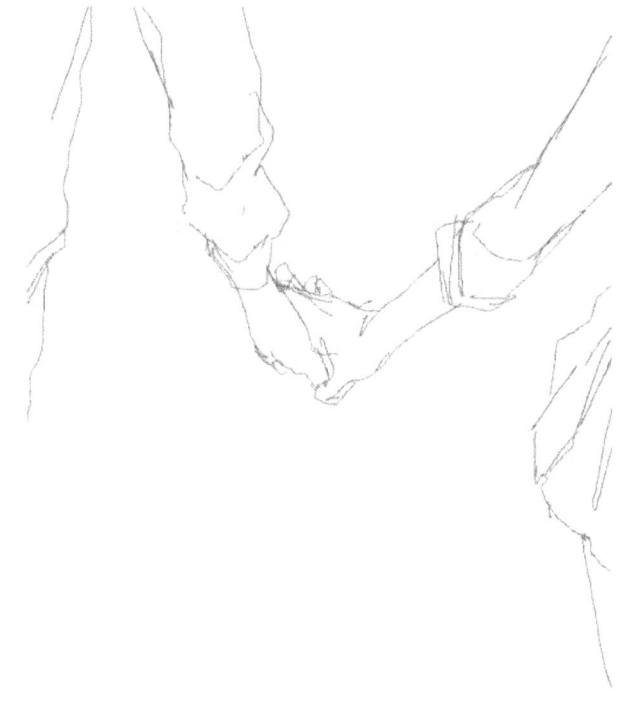

I've started digging a garden in my heart,
Planting flowers and watering them
With all the love that you give me

My heart is no longer a barren land

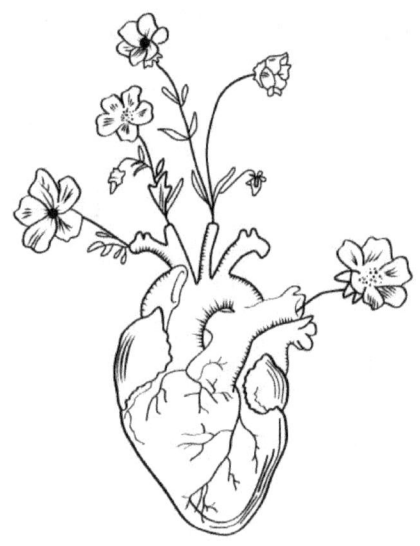

How could this not be?
When the moment that I saw you, my heart skipped a beat
In a room full of people all I saw was you
I had to get you
My heart told me that it was you
You did not reject me
You opened up and accepted me with arms wide open
As if you had been waiting for me too
Did I promise to look for you in lifetimes before?
Your face filled with recognition as if we had laid in bed together
And made a pinkie promise that in each lifetime
We would find each other
You have always been mine
Then and now

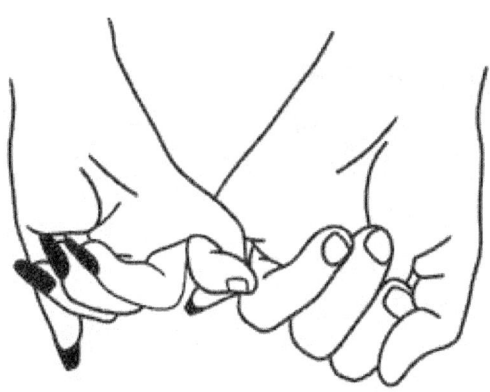

He said that I should find the places
Where he was the most broken
And to love him there
So I kissed him on every part of his body
Found a way to get inside
Made my way through his veins
Like an antibiotic
Healing him from within
He also gets hurt, he feels pain too
But I want to act like medicine
That cures any pain
To make him believe in love again
I want him to feel that I love him
That he is worthy to be loved
He does not have to act tough
Or man up
My love says that he can be vulnerable
Enough to show me
And when life gets tough,
I'll be by his side

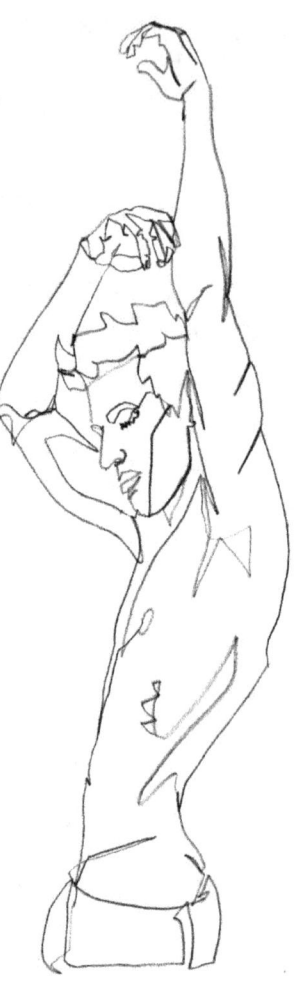

The fear of FALLING in love has always scared me
Because I was unable to trust
That the person I fell for would catch me.
Sounds like an overused cliché right?

But I was so afraid of it that walls on the inside
Did not feel enough to keep the love out
I created a façade on the outside,
Telling anyone that met me not to love me.
"I hate love or the idea of love" was my favourite escape.
"I do not believe in love" was my next best
But it's so funny how love works.

One day when you least expect it in the midst of a storm
Someone comes and offers you an umbrella.
You might have gotten so used to the rain
That you didn't even realise that it was making you sick
But someone comes and shows you
How brightly the sun can shine.
This person comes breaking down walls,
Allowing you to remove the mask and sees you naked
And still thinks you're amazing.

YOU

This flawed human that never needed anyone.
You realise that the air feels lighter,
You're breathing better and you no longer fight it.
You forget why you refused love in the first place,
You forgive your father for not showing you
What love should be like
And you understand that a woman does not have to do
Everything on her own, like your mother.
You stop making people pay for the mistakes of others
And all it took was opening up to receive love.

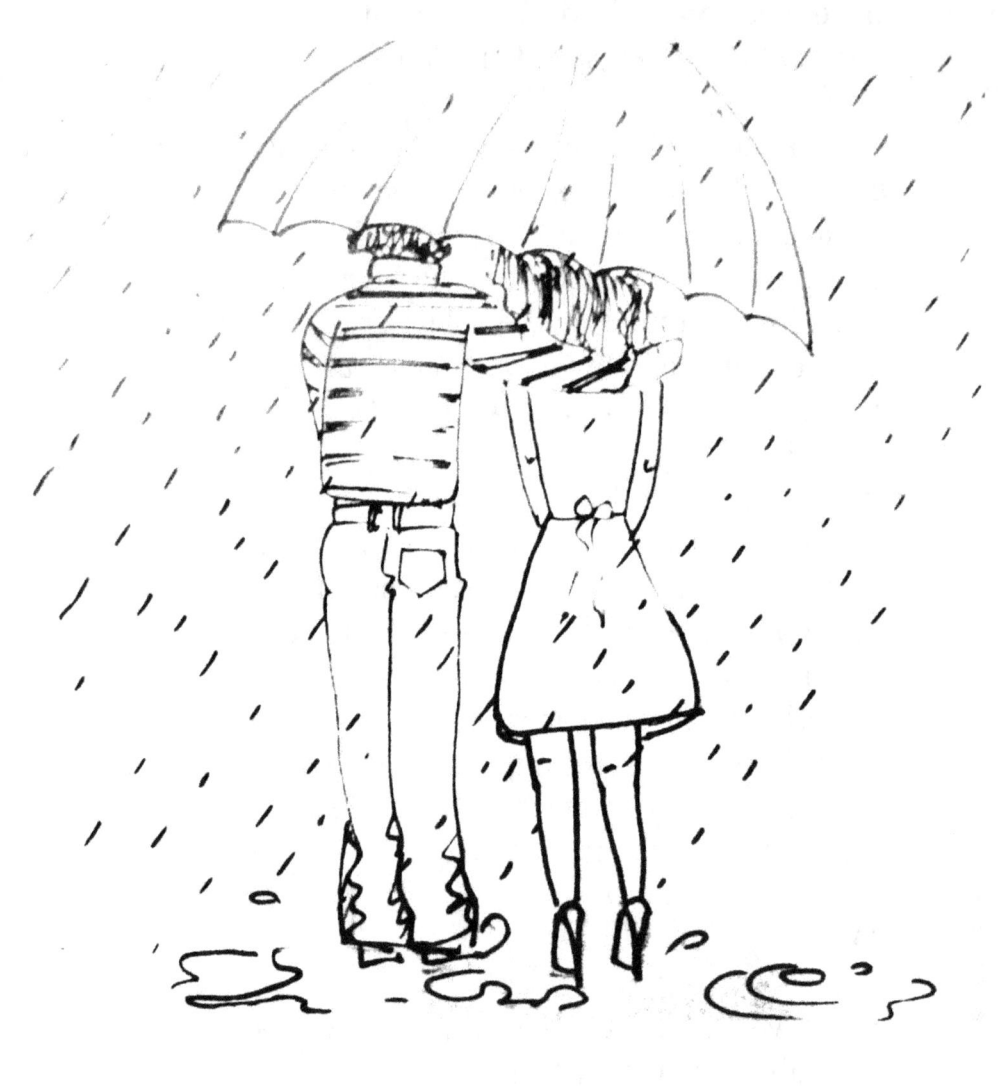

You
watered
me
until
I
opened
up
like
a
flower
blooming
in
the
spring

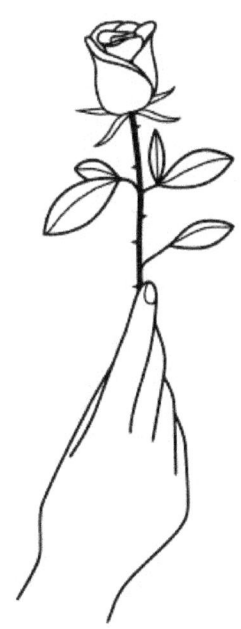

You have reached the end.
Thank you for helping me to remove the mask,
The act and allowing me to stand naked before you.

About the writer: Haseena Saley is a Communication graduate who also has a certificate in teaching. When she is not teaching, she spends her time writing and contemplating life in its various dimensions. This is her first book and most of her pieces are shared on social media where she has a small following. Removing the mask was important for her because she wanted to open up and be seen as a writer who has faced struggle but is trying to overcome it.

Disclaimer: All pictures used in this book were downloaded online and some might be subject to copyright. I (Haseena), do not own any of the pictures illustrated in the book. They were put there to enhance the reader's experience as it relates to the poems and its message. Book cover artwork by Namrata Agarwal
No copyright infringement is intended